This is a simple guide that will get you started on your personal path to success. If you wanted a magic pill that would suddenly put success in your hands, this is not it. If you wanted to spend a lot of money on a detailed step by step guide with hundreds of pages of instructions to follow, detailed performance charts and multi-level checklists, you've gotten the wrong book. But if you are the kind of person who can wake up, pick a task for the day and work on it without drifting off to the water-cooler or the internet this is the book for you.

This book takes away the rhetoric and the 'bafflegab' and opens the portal to profitable business ideas and, if necessary, easy ways to get the funding you need to start your business or expand the one you own

2014 – Excellence-Success Publishing-
www.Excellence –Success.com

CREATE A BUSINESS

Become your own Success Story TODAY!

Believe it or not, you can open your own business and make it successful without being tied up with complicated franchise regulations, or victim to high interest loans.

Most business ideas, from restaurants to retailers are workable if you make the commitment to put time into it. An 'on-line only' business will require your electronic availability, but not necessarily your physical presence; whereas a retail outlet or restaurant may require you being there twenty hours a day, for the first five years. No matter which business style you choose, the reward will be a source of income you control.

How many times have you unwrapped a chicken sandwich and wondered what the poor bird did to make people treat it this way. How many times have you looked at a wilted, limp salad and had to determine the age by carbon-dating? If this is the type of thing that bothers you, maybe you should start a restaurant.

How many times have you had to spend your entire day off driving miles away to get a product or service because there are no stores near you? How many times have you searched the web for a product or service and not found a helpful link?
Did you or do you own a franchise and feel like you are just another employee? Do you want to take your existing business to a new profit level? Do you need to get out of the house and do something?

A small retail shop or cafe may be a perfect business for you. You decide the location, you decide the hours, you decide the decorating design, and you can even decide what your staff will wear. A gift shop or organic 'craft food' establishment is the perfect business to allow you to get rid of the stress of office competition or the boredom of inaction.

You can work with the people you want, select merchandise or design the menu to suit yourself, and change the décor whenever you feel like it because you are the only person who has to approve!

Starting with a small investment, you can own the establishment of your dreams, and when it comes time, you will be the one with a successful business to franchise. With careful planning, your successful business can make as much income from franchise fees as the actual operation.

1. The first thing you need to do is decide on a company name. Once you have done that it is time to insert that name into your business plan.

2. The next thing you need is a business plan. You can hire a lawyer or a business professional to design one for you, or you can buy the software and design one yourself.

3. Find a location: If you have been thinking about opening a 'brick and mortar' business, you probably already have a location in mind. If you do not, then you need to invest some of your time to pinpoint a good location. Don't just decide on a place because it has the equipment you need installed. Be cautious: the equipment could be old, faulty, or just so crusted in years of filth it will be too costly to get clean.

4. When checking out a location, make certain to check what the local municipality plans for the area. Chances are that if you open an upscale French restaurant in a building where zoning was just approved for an outpatient counseling facility for violent offenders, once that facility is opened, the business in your restaurant will fall off. And by the same token, if you open a fast-food- 'greasy spoon' diner in a strip mall already occupied by four of the biggest fast-food franchises in the world, chances are you will close three weeks after you open.

5. Don't open a jewelry boutique next to a chain store that will undercut your prices; don't open your gift shop next to a 'Harry and David'. If you are focusing on gourmet and specialty food items, however, you best bet may be to open next to a 'chain' supermarket. Don't kill yourself with competition before you open.

6. Once you have decided on a prime location, locate three other locations that you could use. That way, if the first one is rented before you get you funding, you still have a choice.

7. If you already own a retail outlet and you want to add features to increase business, take a walk and visit every business within three blocks and see what items they have added as shopping incentives. Do you see a pattern? Add a similar service or product. Something as easy as heart shaped ice cubes in a specialty drink will give customers a reason to come back to your shop more often.

Fund Your Business

Get the cash you need to open or expand, quickly!

Regular people rarely have a rich relative to rely on. Few of people have both somehow saved enough to get started on your own, and managed to hold onto it through the recent financial troubles.

You will need funding to get started and to start, and you will need some kind of funding. Funding can come from many sources, but unless it is coming out of your own pocket, people will want to see that you have a viable plan before investing, loaning, or gifting you money.

1. Refine your business plan. Double check your costs. If you are selling retail, discover three suppliers of every item you stock and get a firm price commitment from at least one of them. Customers stop coming if you are always out of their size. Restaurants close because their supply chain suddenly dries up. Internet businesses fail when they forget to renew their domain names. Don't let your restaurant suffer because the bakery that makes your buns burned down, and don't let your customers

leave because they average size 14 and you don't carry larger than a 12.

2. Get business cards. They do not have to be fancy. A business card introduces you and represents you when you leave. When you hand a person a business card it announces that you KNOW how to handle business. Practice this phrase: *I am a successful business owner, here is my card. Call me if you need anything.* Give a card to everyone. That means your bank teller and the pizza delivery. Leave them in the 'free dinner' jars at the restaurants you visit.

3. Form your company. Although the forms are usually available through your state website (*which will be listed on-line as the name of your state with a www prefix and a .gov suffix*) *click on any tab that says 'business'*. The forms and regulations for each state differ, and the business laws can change yearly.

SELF FINANCING:
- If you've been saving up for something special, what is more special than your own business? The first investment is your own time. Sit down and make a list of pro's and con's. More con's than pros? Then it is time to admit that you LIKE your career and to stop speculating about what could have been. But if you have a long column of pro's take a look at your assets. If you have a

hefty retirement account, ample equity in your home, or even a boat that is eating up marina fees, all of these are assets that you can use to finance your dream.

- If you are planning to become an Internet Reseller or an Affiliate Marketer, you may be able to begin with an investment of $500.00 or less. With no need to rent space, all you need is a computer, a website, an email address, and a mailing list.

RICH RELATIVE:
- Your Great Aunt Sue wants to give you a no-interest start up loan to start your business. This is an excellent turn of events. You still need a business plan, a lawyer and an accountant. Look for a lawyer who is also an accountant. Based on your business plan, have your lawyer draw up a contract and have your accountant get your business license. Once you get your federal Tax ID number, you can open a bank account, deposit the loan and start following your business plan.

CROWDFUNDING:
- This is a relatively new concept, but it involves putting your business plan on a website such as *www.crowdfunder.com*. You then ask the public to fund your 'Project' by telling them how much you need to raise and what they get (usually a mention on the company website or a discount on products) for helping to support you. This is not a loan; you don't need to pay the money back if the

business fails. But there are rules in place to prevent the person who raises $10,000 to start an organic farm from buying a new car instead.

- Crowd Funding is also done on a smaller scale for creative projects or 'one time only' projects. Gofundme.com will help you raise enough money to cover the expense of printing a cookbook.. Upstart.com and Equitynet.com will help you start a small specialty business such as a restaurant. Fundrise.com is perfect for people with ideas in real estate and Fundly.com will let you entertain all possible ideas. If you can write a short, heartfelt and convincing promotional piece about you and your ideas, you will get funding in as little as 30 days.

BANK LOAN:
- Your Local Banker is the next step. Review your business plan carefully and be prepared to produce up to 5 years of personal tax returns. You will more than likely be asked to put up the business, your home, or both as collateral on a 10 year start up loan.

PRIVATE INVESTORS:
- If you find yourself able to raise part of the investment money, but not all, it is time to think about bringing in friends and family as investors. This means that, in return for giving you part of the startup cash, that person will own that portion of your business. If they give you half, they own half.

If they own half, they get half of the profit. And that means, unless you agree on something else, that person gets half even if they do not set foot inside the doors. This may not be a bad thing. You can also use a combination of many investors. A good business incorporation company will provide you with the tools you need to issue stock in your business in return for investment capital. A good lawyer will provide the guidance you need.

PUBLIC INVESTORS:
- Business websites like b2b.thetradepost.com are available for businesses to buy and sell all products. A chance to invest money in a new business is a product that can be sold. Read the instructions on the website. A basic membership is free. Post your investment contract details, including your expected 5 year profits, and be prepared to send copies of your business plan to interested people. It may take several months to find investment capital, but one you have it you are ready for the next step. This may not be a bad thing. You can also use a combination of many investors. A good business incorporation company will provide you with the tools you need to issue stock in your business in return for investment capital.

INVESTMENT REQUIREMENTS

You will need to have some money to start your business. We have evaluated the most common expenses and listed them here. Not every person will have all of these expenses. If your business is 'internet-only' you will have no need of signs and cash-registers. If you are working alone, you won't need to pay hiring fees. When you develop your business plan, you should use these expenses as a guide and add or subtract when necessary.

1. **Website and E-mail**: Regardless of the type of business you plan to open, you will need to have a website and an email address. If you plan to be an on-line business, this is an absolute must. You will need a multipage website, domain, and an SSL certificate in addition to someone with the knowledge and expertise to run it for you. Many companies offer a complete service, including the e-commerce which allows you to get paid. If you feel insecure about running your own website, consider using a service like GoDaddy.com or Intuit. You may be able to get a one page website for as little as $80.00 per year

but a multipage website with full design service and support may cost you $5,000.00 per year or more.

2. **Security Deposit and Rent**: Based on an average of $2,333.00 per month plus paying the first and last month's rent in advance - $7,000.00 not only gets you in, but keeps you secure while you renovate. In some cases, the landlord will do so much of the preliminary work that only the signage and decorating are left.

3. **Leasehold Improvements**: If the landlord won't do it for you, you need to do it yourself. Don't cut corners. Every day you are not open is a day you lose money. Don't plan on doing it all yourself. You are going to be busy with other tasks. Nothing beats a good, experienced general contractor. Get three estimates and settle on a final contract that requires no more than 30% down payment before work starts. Reserve $1,000.00 to pay out as a bonus for completing the work ahead of schedule.

4. **Business Licensing and Inspections**: In addition to a Federal Tax number, you will need to be in compliance with the codes of your own state. If you hired a lawyer or a CPA they will have taken care of these details for you, If you are handling these items yourself, go to your state website, download and submit all forms with whatever payments are required so you will have all of your operating licenses framed and on the wall before your opening day. Be prepared to spend $100.00 to $500.00 to make yourself legally compliant with all local laws.

5. **Interior Design**: If you don't hire a professional firm to do this task, then take your time to do a little research on the effects of color on customers. You want people to walk in, feel welcome and leave feeling in a good mood. So, unless you are going for a specific theme and effect, with your products being secondary, then don't paint your store black and dress your staff in strobe lights.

6. **Exterior and Interior Signage**: Talk to a sign professional. Choose an established company and not a franchise that will slap together a sign on a dime. You need your name over the door and it needs to be permanent. No one can read a faded sign rolling down the road at 30mph. A good sign professional can give you good suggestions about what will work best in your area and be able to duplicate your theme both inside and out.

7. **Equipment and Furniture**: If you were lucky enough to buy out a location with usable furniture and equipment then you can spend your budget on cleaning, maintenance and upgrades. A visit to a local upholstery store will provide fabric for curtains and other décor. It may be the only things you need are storage shelves and a filing system. A quick trip to your local office product discounter will yield everything you need.

8. **Cash Registers, POS System and Software:** Intuit, the maker of Turbo Tax, QuickBooks and Quicken, is probably the best small business software on the market. Contact the company for information on the cash-register systems that incorporate QuickBooks software to record

the sales and make the daily bookkeeping tasks easy. Properly set up, all sales are recorded directly into your QuickBooks ledger, and what is even better, at the end of the business period, QuickBooks data is easily exported into Turbo Tax so you can file your taxes. This way you will have everything taken care of from payroll to careful inventory tracking without having to keep a full time bookkeeper on staff. Using this system will save you money.

9. **Miscellaneous Hiring Fees:** Even if you have people all lined up, you may have to hire a few people at the last moment. Although you can search Craig's List for free, businesses must pay a small fee to advertise. Set aside enough to cover several weeks of advertising expenses.

10. **Merchandise:** Food is perishable. If you are starting a restaurant a lot of the food items you will use will need to be purchased daily. For all other businesses make certain that you have vendors under contract who will make weekly or even daily deliveries of the products you need. If you plan to market products for an affiliate partner you won't have this expense.

11. **Miscellaneous Fees:** This is cash you need to have available for the small items you may have forgotten. These could be, but are not limited to – Condo fees, trash pickup, special recycling, utility deposits, rodent inspection and green energy fees.

12. **Franchise Fees:** While start-up franchise operations may have to pay up to 70% of their weekly profits to a parent company in order to operate, as the owner of your own,

original establishment, you will never have to pay even one penny of your income out as a franchise fee.

13. **Grand Opening Advertising Blitz**: Make people want your product before you open. Hire a good PR firm before you launch to get your name out there. Get an e-mail list and get you message out! Make certain you also use social networking sites like Facebook, Yelp and Twitter and consider starting a blog. Do not forget to list your company with 'Groupon' and 'Living Social' if they are in your area.

14. **Three Weeks Payroll**: Including payroll taxes. Chances are that your business will do average to good business during the first few weeks. People like new experiences, so you will probably 'break even' meaning payroll shouldn't be an issue. But nature is fickle. A week of rainstorms, snow or even 100 degree heat can throw a business off. Remember, your employees are dependent on you. If they were independently wealthy <u>they wouldn't be working in your store</u>. If you make certain they get paid at the same time every week, and if they see you bending over backward to make a success, they will work even harder for you. After all, when you open the second location, the management is going to come from the people already on your staff.

Employee Expenses per Week

If you have employees, you must pay them. Even if you are starting a family business, and the only employees will be family members, you need to make the provision to pay them.

You will see the included chart is a breakdown of the weekly expenses associated with the 16 employees necessary to run a retail business.

1. **Employee Type:** Title, position, and job description of the employee.

2. **Days Worked:** Hourly assignment

3. **Total Hours:** For budgeting purposes these hours are assigned to the employees. Once your business is open, you may wish to adjust them based on customer flow.

4. **Per Hour:** Hourly Wage that you pay the employee. You may wish to adjust these figures based on your state's minimum wage laws.

5. **Per Week:** This is the basic weekly expense per employee. However there are other expenses associated with employees that most people forget.

6. **Benefits:** If you want happy and hardworking employees, you need to offer benefits. A basic, minimum health package will cost $25.00 per week for a full time employee.

7. **Payroll Taxes:** Although the taxes are withheld from the employees' paychecks, the employer has to match the withholding amount for Social Security and Medicare. This is the average cost per employee type. Check with your state tax authority for the exact percentage rate for your locale.

8. **Unemployment Insurance:** This is the average cost per employee type per week. Check with your state tax authority for the exact percentage rate for your locale.

9. **Total Employee Expense:** This is the total cost to you per employee per week

Based on this spread sheet, the total weekly employee costs would be $5,700. Once you copy this data onto your own spreadsheet, you will be able to adjust these figures and add your own calculations to customize your expenses and insert into a final business plan.

Employee Expenses Per Week - Average

Employee Type	Days Worked	Total Hours	Per hour	Per Week	Benefits	Payroll ITaxes	Unemp. Ins.	Total Empl. Exp.
Primary Opening Manager	mon-fri 9:30am to 6:30pm	45	16.50	742.50	$25.00	56.80	14.85	839.15
Weekday Opening Staff	mon-fri 10am to 6pm	35	10.00	350.00	$25.00	26.78	7.00	408.78
Weekday Opening Staff	mon-fri 10am to 6pm	35	10.00	350.00	$25.00	26.78	7.00	408.78
Weekend Opening Staff	Sat & Sun 10am to 6pm	14	10.00	140.00	$0.00	10.71	2.80	153.51
Weekend Opening Staff	Sat & Sun 10am to 6pm	14	10.00	140.00	$0.00	10.71	2.80	153.51
Total Weekly Payroll				2,001.50	$100.00	153.11	40.03	2,294.64

START AN INTERNET BASED BUSINESS

YOU have what it takes to run a profitable internet based business from home!

A personally inspired web based enterprise is the perfect business for you if both your time and investment funds are limited. Your location is on the web so you don't need to worry about finding office space, and you set your own hours so you can work from anywhere and at any time. You simply carry your pad with you and you are always ready to start working.

No employees' are necessary, so you can choose to operate as a sole proprietorship and save yourself a monthly accounting expense and certain federal taxes. If you have decided to use your web enterprise to transition out of your current job without giving up the income, the ability to work from anywhere is very important. If you currently own a franchise or work in a retail store, a web based business is perfect for your needs.

If you have limited familiarity with the internet, the prospect of opening an internet business may be both attractive and daunting. Even if your goal is to put your existing business on the web, you may not be certain how this will help you will make a profit. You need a business idea; a website; products; payment processing; domain name; web hosting and especially advertising. All of these things together can seem like a huge obstacle, but in reality, it is very easy to get started on the road to success.

You don't need to pay either a business consultant or an expensive web design company to start you on the road to success. Everyone wants a shiny new website with interesting gimmicks, and there are companies that will do it for a fee. But if you follow this advice, you can save yourself thousands of dollars in startup fees and avoid the frustration of falling prey to one of those companies that are only available if you agree to an expensive contract.

You will have no trouble starting your internet business with an investment of under $300.00. Any person willing to use their head, and put in some time can be successful. The tools are all, right there on-line for anyone to use. For example Godaddy.com is one of the world's largest domain registrars and web hosting providers. But what people don't pay attention to is the fact that for a $9.99 domain registration fee, you can get the dot com you've always wanted. Then for only $120.00 a year, you get a 900+ page website, free web hosting, a 1,000 address battery of email addresses that can be established for your website and an SSL certificate for security. Even if you can't think of what to do immediately with your website, they will broker your website as a 'parking spot' for advertising and this will allow your website to generate income while you decide on what to do with it.

Finally, a well named website has resale value. So if you buy the domain and website, and you park advertising on it, and then you decide to do something else, you can usually auction it off at a profit. With careful planning, your website can be valuable for the name alone. You can click here to get started immediately!

Choosing a Business:

The first thing you need to do is make a business plan and to do that you must decide on a business. Are you an advice column or an entertainment magazine? Are you selling a product or an idea? Are you using the website as a portal to a brick and mortar business or are you using it to promote ideas? Below is a list of businesses that you can easily manage as an internet business:

1. **Product Reseller:** *This is retail without having to maintain an inventory. There are many product resellers that require no up-front investment at all. If you do not already have a relationship with the supplier, contact product wholesalers through the numerous b2b business websites on line. Next, conclude an agreement for the supplier to 'drop ship' product directly to the customer for you and bill you on shipment for the wholesale cost. On your website you will list the full retail plus shipping and handling. Since your product expenses and income are occurring at close to the same time; your start up exposure is usually limited. Double check your contracts to further minimize your costs. Discover three suppliers of every item you 'stock' and get a firm price commitment from them before you begin.*

2. **Information/Entertainment Marketer:** *You don't need to know a Hollywood star to write about entertainment news. You only need to write well. Combine witty stories*

with public domain photos and you have an 'on line entertainment magazine'. If your expertise is astrology, write about that and include pictures of your specific tools. If you are an adult with exhibitionist leanings, you can put that talent to work, too. The idea is to identify your areas of expertise and offer them up with a professional looking flair. Give people what they want: insights, entertainments and quips. Incorporate pictures, diagrams and an e-mail forum where you answer questions. 'Tweet' with them, and they will come back hourly. Advertise your primary business, that of a friend, or approach local merchants and offer a business card ad on your website for a pre-agreed amount per year. Create content around products you like and let those advertisers come to you for a per-click deal, or go through an advertising broker. Adult Sites, especially, make money from well-placed, click thru advertising.

3 **Retailer:** If you have been working on crafts for years, the great news is that you have enough items (inventory) to become an on-line retailer already! If not, you will need to decide what you plan to sell and then raise the money to purchase the items. If you want to start a Tee Shirt business, like **Johnny Cupcake**, then you will have to design the tee shirts and get them printed. If you want to sell handmade soaps like **Berry Towne Crafts** you will need to purchase the soap making supplies, and if you want to start a jewelry business like **Aquarius Custom Jewelry** you will need to purchase jewelry making supplies. For every product you can think of, there are also many wholesale outlets that will sell you six dozen or more of an item at an incredible price. Business websites like **http://b2b.thetradepost.com/** are a great resource

for all businesses, especially those who want to buy wholesale. Virtually any item that your purchase, you can then sell on your website at a profit.

4 **Affiliate Marketer:** *If you need to generate a secondary income but you have limited time, space and resources, this is the best way to start. All you need is a one page website with advertising and content, an e-mail address, a mailing list, and accounts with several pay-per-click advertising affiliates and marketing partners. Your* **affiliates** *will generally be on line advertising brokers who want you to put their code on your website so they can sell that advertising space to their customers. They then pay you a commission every time someone clicks through to one of their customers and a higher commission every time someone clicks through and BUYS something. Your marketing partner will be a company that provides you with a product or products at no charge and you then feature it on your website or on an on-line store they provide for you free. These products are 'click through'. The companies that do this do all of the work for you - from manufacturing to warehousing and shipping. You promote the products and they send you the commission from every sale.*

Planning Your Business:

The plan does not need to start with a complex document generated by an MBA or a CPA. You hire a business specialist after your company is making money. Right now you need a pen and a piece of paper. Go get these important tools because it is time to get to work.

- Write the type of internet business you are planning to start; Resale, Information or Retail across the top. Next, write your first choice for a name for your business. Now underneath, write several alternatives to use in case your business name is already being used.

- Write the type of product you have decided to market for income. If it is information, what type of information? Once you decide write it down. The same holds true if you are reselling a product or retailing a product. When you begin, try to limit yourself to one product line: Clothing, Electronics; Crafts; Food Items; Auto Parts or any item you feel you have enough experience with to sell to others.

- Research the places you will use to get your product. If you are selling information, and you are not an expert, do you know someone who is? Can you do the research yourself to become an expert? Are you experienced enough to provide the information plus references to experts? Find this out and write it down. Similarly, if you are selling a product, do you have three reliable suppliers of that product? Do the product research, find the suppliers and write them down.

Putting Your Website Together:

Now that you have your website planned on paper, you have to put it together.

- *If you are creating an information website, you will need to assemble the information you plan to make public. You either need to write articles and stories, pay people to write them for you, or locate a company that will sell you pre-written articles for a fee. There are companies that have a staff of content writers that you can subscribe to for a fee: Content Factory, Writer Access, Media Shower, Text Master, Website Text etc. You can also hire college students - graduate teaching assistants and other 'borderline' professionals to write articles for you. 4 cents per word for a 500 page article is the going rate. Ask around: you may have a friend or acquaintance who fancies himself a writer.*

- *You may need pictures, and videos, so you will either need to create them, pay people to create them for you, or find public domain art that you can re-publish for a fee. Once you have your articles and pictures you need to decide which page of your website will be best for them.*

- *If you are a retailer or reseller, your job is a lot easier. You just need pictures of your product and a description. Your supplier will usually be happy to provide you with jpeg files of the products you buy along with written catalog descriptions. You only need to decide where to put them on your website. If you are selling your own products, you will need to take a clear picture of each item you are selling, and write a catchy description yourself.*

Launching Your Website:

This is the easy part of what you plan to do! You may have been lucky enough to get free website software with your computer. If you have it, use that free software to get your business started. If you don't have easy to use, free software, or you find what you have is confusing, you do not have to worry. GoDaddy.com is one of the domain registration and Web hosting companies that make the entire set up easy with products like 'Website Tonite'. They provide free customer support for their products, and they can do your complete web design and set up for a reasonable fee. If you have an existing business and you have been using business products like QuickBooks, Intuit.com has website packages you might prefer.

Making Money with Your Website:

You have your website up and running with content and at least 3 ads per page. You have an e-mail account associated with your website. You have an e-mail mailing list of 10,000 names. Everyone in your personal network has something on their Facebook page, blog or website that points out or links to your website. You have several affiliate partners with ads on your pages. You have one to three marketing partners who are giving you the profit from every item sold and you have an account for the money to go into. You are now ready to create income

- *Flex your earning muscles and get yourself paid. Retailing and reselling have an easy cash flow to follow. If you had a storefront in a mall, people would walk in with money and walk out with their purchase. Instead you need to plan to do a little bit of internet advertising. Google's Advertising is the best place to start.*
- *You will need affiliate partners. Good companies to work with are Google Ad Sense, Go Daddy, Amazon.com*

Associates, Click Bank, Link Share, Share a Sale, FastCard Tech, PayPal/Bill Me Later, Commission Junction and there are others. You can usually join for free. They provide you code for ads that you then put on your website. When people click on those ads, you get paid.

- *Now you have to let everyone know that you are open for business. Start by preparing the first email that you will send out. Style it as a friendly letter or as an offer they cannot live without. You know your audience. If the first mailing does not get a good response, change it for the next one. One Word Of Caution: WATCH YOUR SPELLING! People seem to think that bad spelling from an email vendor means the vendor is in India and has ties to the Russian Mob. You want people to read your email and click, so YOU get PAID!*

- *Of you have decided to use a marketing partner, try: Spoonflower.com, Cafepress.com, Zazzle.com, Spreadshirt.com, Pikistore.com, Tastebook.com,, Createspace.com, Blurb.com, Lulu.com, Gamecrafter.com, Ponoko.com, Shapeways.com, Imagekind.com and Deviantart.com. They are the best. But you can contact the manufacturer of any product you personally like and ask them for the code that you can put on your website to link to their products and get a per click commission. If you have a friend or acquaintance that has a business and has products they want to promote, you can make a partnership with them, too.*

You need to manage your funds, and a great way to do this is with a Pay Pal account. PayPal allows people to purchase what they want from you using a credit card, cash or check, but relieves you of the burden of tracking a lot of different payment types. If you have an Information and entertainment website, you will probably rely solely on advertising for income.

- Go on line and set up a Pay Pal account that is connected to a bank account you plan to only use for business.

- Once Your Pay Pal account is activated, they will provide you with 'Buy Now' buttons that you can add to the descriptions of each product on your website.

- If you want to make extra income from your retail website, you can also run advertising for other companies. It is easy to place per click ads, on your existing website, and you can become a Go Daddy or Google advertising partner. Don't forget to contact your local businesses. They may also be interested in paying you a fee for advertising.

For reasons unknown to even the best business professionals, even the best run and best funded businesses fail. It could be the location, it could be the employees, it could be the product, it could be the competition it could be all of those factors or new and unknown factors. This business advice is an outline for your to follow, but in no way guarantees success in your venture. Your success is 100% up to you. Ecellence-Success.com; and all related individuals/entities are in no way responsible any type of failure, lack of income, loss of income, litigation, loss, misdeed, unfortunate incident or anything that results from your use of any kind of information, including business advice, and/ or any suggestions on this or any other related website.

www.Excellence-Success.com

www.ingramcontent.com/pod-product-compliance
Lightning Source LLC
Chambersburg PA
CBHW041612180526
45159CB00002BC/816